contents

	page
Introduction	i
Part One: The notes we play	1
Part Two: How the notes are written	5
Part Three: The length of the notes	7
Part Four: Bars	9
Part Five: Reading rhythms	13
Part Six: Which notes to play	15
Part Seven: Other symbols	21
Part Eight: What next?	23
Index	25

acknowledgments

Many thanks to Simon, Ros, Matt and Zoe for all their suggestions and support, and to Iffig for the Snap Man!

Introduction

This book covers the basic concepts of reading music and music theory, and has been compiled in response to questions from adult students of traditional music. I have been searching for a reference book to recommend to students, but have not yet found one - most are either aimed at children, are too complex for the beginner or are based on the classical music exam structure. I hope that this will help to fill the void.

This book does not aim to encourage students to replace or ignore the other fundamental aspects of learning traditional music. A tune on paper is merely the skeleton of the music. It rarely gives any information about features of style such as phrasing, ornamentation, variation and speed, and even if it did, this information would be someone else's interpretation of the music. Traditional music is fluid and personal, and musicians should take care to use their ears much more than their eyes in exploring the range of possibilities for playing a tune.

Although it is perfectly possible to play and enjoy traditional tunes without reading music, written music has become widely used by traditional musicians searching out new tunes, in books or on the Internet. We don't often have the luxury of learning tunes by ear directly from other musicians other than in formal workshops, and written music is a useful jog to the memory. It is also helpful to have a basic understanding of how it all works when talking about musical ideas with others.

The traditional music I am describing is western European traditional music and its close relatives in North America. I have tried to keep explanations as free of musical jargon as possible, and to explain any words and terms as they appear. I hope singers will understand my use of the word "instrument", by which I mean the voice as well. I have also suggested topics for further investigation in some of the chapters; information about these can be found in other books, on the Internet or from your teacher.

Don't try and digest all the information at once! The book is designed as a reference tool to be used alongside lessons or workshops, and it may take some time for it all to sink in.

Sarah Northcott, August 2006.

part one: the notes we play

The notes we play in traditional music are usually named and written down using the Western classical music system. Generally this works well, but there are occasions when traditional music doesn't quite fit with the classical system, and these will be highlighted as they arise.

To explain the system of notes it is helpful to look at how the classical music system has developed. This is illustrated using diagrams which show part of the piano/accordion keyboard.

THE NAMING OF THE NOTES - STAGE ONE

In the first stage of the modern system, the notes were named using the letters **A** to **G**.

THE OCTAVE
The pattern of notes is able to repeat itself because notes of the same name played together *sound like the same note*, even though one is higher in pitch than the other. The gap between a note and the next note upwards or downwards of the same name is called an **octave** (so called because it was originally made up of eight notes, including the starting note). This is shown on Keyboard 1 (below) using the note A, but it applies to any two notes of the same name. This keyboard has no black notes - they arrive in the next stage.

KEYBOARD 1

| A | B | C | D | E | F | G | A | B | C | D | E | F | G | A | B |

T S T T S T T T S T T S T T T

T = tone, S = semitone

1

TONES AND SEMITONES

Classical music measures the gaps between notes (or the size of the jump from one note to the next) in **tones** (or **whole steps**) and **semitones** (or **half steps**). Two semitones equal one tone.

It is important to understand that the gaps or jumps between the notes on Keyboard 1 *are not all the same size.*

On Keyboard 1, the tone steps (T) and semitone steps (S) are marked. The pattern is the always the same for notes of the same letter, so the gap between A and B is always a tone. **There are always two places at this stage where the gap is only a semitone - between B and C and between E and F.**

THE NAMING OF THE NOTES - STAGE TWO

In the next stage, the black notes on the piano were gradually added to the range of notes played. These extra notes were added between two notes which were a tone apart, therefore adding semitone steps in between. The black notes were *not* added between B and C or between E and F because the gap between these notes was already only a semitone. This created an even pattern of twelve semitones in the octave, shown on Keyboard 2 (below) using A to A as an example. This applies to all octaves.

KEYBOARD 2

THE NEW NOTE NAMES - SHARPS AND FLATS

The new notes were given names using the symbols # (**sharp**) and ♭ (**flat**).

A sharp raises the pitch of a note by a semitone.

A flat lowers the pitch of a note by a semitone.

Most notes now have two possible names. Keyboard 3 (below) shows all the possible names of notes. The note names shown in brackets are those least likely to be used in traditional music. Don't worry about which name to use at the moment, but do try to understand the pattern of notes, particularly the semitone gaps between B and C and between E and F.

KEYBOARD 3

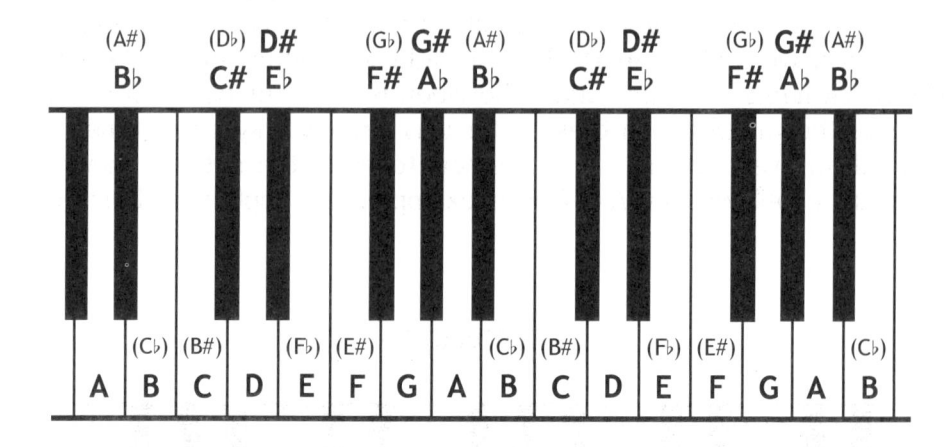

| (A#) | (D♭) **D#** | (G♭) **G#** (A#) | (D♭) **D#** | (G♭) **G#** (A#) |
| **B♭** | **C#** **E♭** | **F# A♭ B♭** | **C#** **E♭** | **F# A♭ B♭** |

| A | B | C | D | E | F | G | A | B | C | D | E | F | G | A | B |

(C♭) (B#) (F♭) (E#)   (C♭) (B#) (F♭) (E#)   (C♭)

THE NATURAL

The other symbol you will find next to a note is ♮ or **natural**. This is used to cancel any previous instruction about the note. For example, earlier in a tune there was a G#; if the next G to be played is an ordinary G, the natural symbol will be found next to the G note, cancelling the sharp.

Not all traditional instruments use all of these notes (e.g. pipes, whistles, some melodeons) so make sure you know which notes are found on your instrument. Some traditions use other notes in between those shown (known as *microtones*), and these can only be played on instruments where the notes aren't fixed (e.g. voice, fiddle etc.) or instruments designed to have the extra notes (e.g. some keyboards used in Middle Eastern music). It is difficult to write these down, so there's no substitute for learning from other musicians - it may be that the music you're reading has been altered slightly to make it possible to write down using the classical system.

Some musicians, often singers, use a system called "solfege" or "sol-fa". There are several variations of this system, and it is based on naming the notes Do, Re, Mi, Fa, Sol, La and Ti (you might know a song about this!) It is useful as it helps singers get to know the jumps or intervals between the notes in a tune. You can translate written music into this system for individual tunes, but you will need some knowledge of **keys** and **scales** to do so (see Part Six).

Some music written for fixed-note instruments (notably pipes) leaves out any reference to sharps or flats because the instrument can only play certain notes, so make sure you know what the notes should be. Highland bagpipe music is written in this way, and you should also be aware that the notes a highland piper actually plays are a little over a semitone higher than the written notes suggest.

for further investigation

If you're interested in physics, the history of musical notes is fascinating. **Pythagoras** studied the properties of notes and harmonics found in the natural world, and discovered not only the physical relationships between them but also a significant problem with these notes for some musicians (known as the Pythagorean Comma). This problem was overcome by **Bach** and others by altering the pitch of notes very slightly, creating the notes our brains are used to hearing today in classical music (a process known as **equal temperament**). Fixed key instruments such as bagpipes tend *not* to be tuned in this way, which is why some of their notes sound unusual - they're not necessarily out of tune!

part two: how the notes are written

The notes are written on a set of five lines called a **stave** or **staff**. Imagine a piano keyboard - it would be impossible to represent all these notes on one line of music in a way that is easy to read, so the notes have been divided into sections and a symbol called a **clef** is used to indicate which section is being used.

The clef most commonly found in traditional music is the **treble clef** or **G clef**:

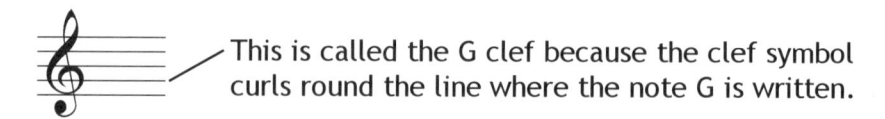

This is called the G clef because the clef symbol curls round the line where the note G is written.

Music for instruments such as the cello which play lower notes is written using the **bass clef** or **F clef**:

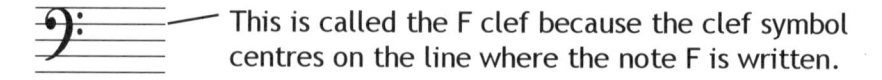

This is called the F clef because the clef symbol centres on the line where the note F is written.

Piano and keyboard music is written using two lines of music, one for each clef (and one for each hand!):

The curly bracket on the left indicates that both lines of music should be played at the same time.

Notes of the same name aren't found in the same place on each clef, so if you're learning to read music for the keyboard or piano you will need to learn two sets of note positions.

There are another set of clefs called **C clefs** which are unique - they move around the five lines to show where the note C is written. These have been devised to cope with instruments and voices that use a range of notes which don't sit comfortably on the treble or bass clefs. Viola music uses a C clef, but you are very unlikely to find traditional music written like this. Just in case, it looks like this:

This is the position of the C clef in viola music.

Here are the notes in the treble clef and the bass clef:

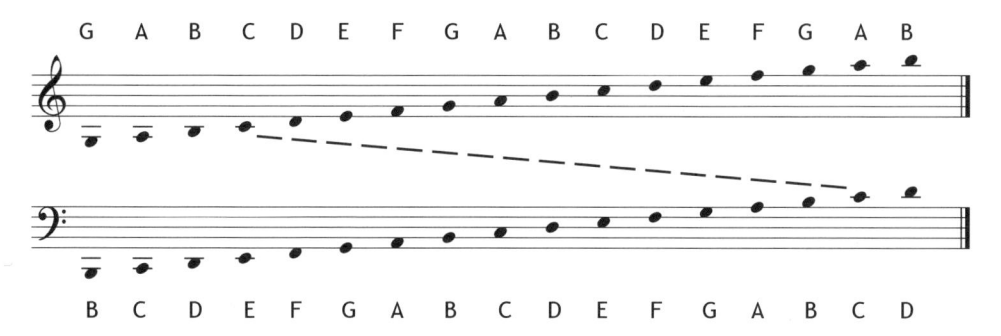

You will see that notes are written beyond the five lines of the stave; the small lines used to add notes above and below the stave are called **leger lines**, and you can add even more leger lines than are shown above. Because these extra notes are added, the clefs overlap - the two C notes joined by the dotted line are exactly the same note, as are the notes shown surrounding the C. This C note is known as **middle C**, because it is the C nearest to the middle of the piano keyboard.

If you are learning an instrument which uses only one of these clefs, you don't need to learn the position of the notes on the other clef. Many song melodies are written in the treble clef, even though you may sing the tune an octave or even two octaves lower in pitch than the notes suggest.

It may help to learn the position of the notes using phrases - try the ones below or make up your own!

> **Every Good Boy Deserves Fruit** - the lines on the treble clef
> **FACE** - the spaces on the treble clef
> **Good Boys Deserve Fine Apples** - the lines on the bass clef
> **All Cows Eat Grass** - the spaces on the bass clef

In order to read music fluently, however, you should learn the notes while playing them on your instrument so that eventually your eye reads the note and this is immediately linked to the physical act of playing or singing that note without your brain consciously processing the information. If you are a singer you will also practice the different jumps or intervals between the notes in a tune as you have no keyboard or fingerboard to help guide you to the note.

part three: the length of the notes

The notes are written using different symbols which show their lengths. The notes below are the most commonly used and have the following

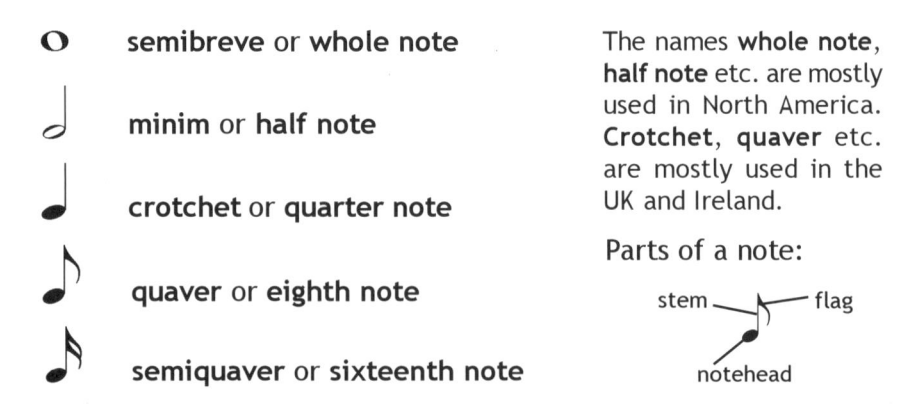

o   **semibreve** or **whole note**

𝅗𝅥   **minim** or **half note**

♩   **crotchet** or **quarter note**

♪   **quaver** or **eighth note**

𝅘𝅥𝅯   **semiquaver** or **sixteenth note**

The names **whole note**, **half note** etc. are mostly used in North America. **Crotchet**, **quaver** etc. are mostly used in the UK and Ireland.

Parts of a note:

stem — flag
notehead

It is important to understand that these different lengths of notes do not in any way show the *speed* at which the whole piece of music is played; they only show the lengths of the notes *in relation to each other*. The relationship between the notes is as follows:

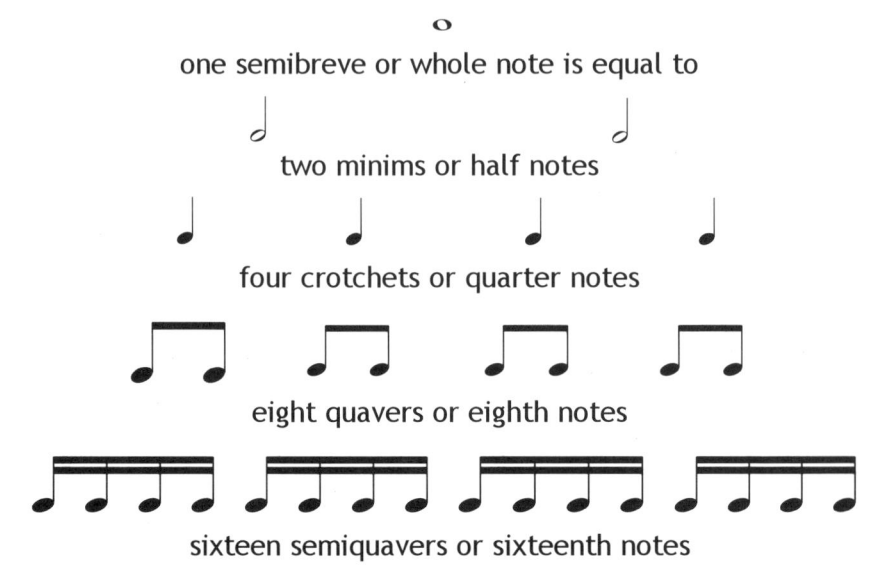

o

one semibreve or whole note is equal to

𝅗𝅥   𝅗𝅥

two minims or half notes

♩   ♩   ♩   ♩

four crotchets or quarter notes

♫ ♫ ♫ ♫

eight quavers or eighth notes

𝅘𝅥𝅯𝅘𝅥𝅯𝅘𝅥𝅯𝅘𝅥𝅯 𝅘𝅥𝅯𝅘𝅥𝅯𝅘𝅥𝅯𝅘𝅥𝅯 𝅘𝅥𝅯𝅘𝅥𝅯𝅘𝅥𝅯𝅘𝅥𝅯 𝅘𝅥𝅯𝅘𝅥𝅯𝅘𝅥𝅯𝅘𝅥𝅯

sixteen semiquavers or sixteenth notes

As you can see, notes with flags can be joined together (normally for one beat of music) using horizontal lines called **beams**. Notes of different lengths can be joined together.

So 𝅗𝅥 = ♩ ♩, ♩ = ♪ ♪ and ♪ = ♬ ♬

Another important type of note is the **dotted note**. Putting a dot after a note increases its length by half as much again:

♩. = ♪ ♪ ♪   A dotted crotchet/quarter note is equal to the length of three quavers/eighth notes.

♪. = ♬ ♬ ♬   A dotted quaver/eighth note is equal to the length of three semiquavers/sixteenth notes.

You will also find notes called **triplets**. These are usually written as three quavers/eighth notes with a "3" above or below, and they are to be played evenly during one crotchet/quarter note beat of music. Each note will be slightly shorter than a quaver, but this is an easy way of writing this rhythm:

$$\overset{3}{\underset{}{♪♪♪}} = ♩$$

There are also symbols for moments of silence, called **rests**. Each type of note has an equivalent rest which represents the same length of time:

𝄻 semibreve or whole note rest   𝄾 quaver or eighth note rest

𝄼 minim or half note rest   𝄿 semiquaver or sixteenth note rest

𝄽 crotchet or quarter note rest

Dotted rests work in the same way as dotted notes, so the dot increases the length of the rest by half as much again:

𝄽. = 𝄾 𝄾 𝄾   which is the same length as ♩.

Playing these different length notes and rests is a matter of learning the note values and counting the beats. Reading different note lengths and rhythms is looked at in detail in Part Five on page 13.

part four: bars

Written music is divided into **bars** (also sometimes known as measures) which give the music its basic rhythmic structure.

TIME SIGNATURES

The number of beats in each bar is shown by the **time signature**, and this also specifies the type of beats in each bar.

The time signature is written at the beginning of the music, and consists of two numbers:

The **top number** indicates the number of beats in the bar.
The **bottom number** shows the kind of beat these are:

  2 represents minims or half notes;
  4 represents crotchets or quarter notes;
  8 represents quavers or eighth notes;
  16 represents semiquavers or sixteenth notes.

You may also come across these symbols:

which represents 4/4 time (also known as common time)

which represents 2/2 time (also known as cut time)

The time signature refers to all the bars in the tune, unless shown otherwise (see Tunes With Bars of Different Lengths on page 10).

The notes in a bar should always add up to the total shown by the time signature. There are many possible combinations of notes.

Using the **3/4** time signature as an example, the notes in the following bars all add up to three crotchets or quarter notes per bar:

4/4 TIME

Here are some examples in **4/4** time (four crotchets per bar). Remember that the triplet in the last bar adds up to one crotchet beat (see page 8):

6/8 TIME

Here are some examples of **6/8** time (six quavers per bar). Tunes in 6/8 time are usually written in two groups of three, giving a rhythm of two main beats per bar (see page 13 for more about this):

PICK-UP OR LEAD NOTES

Often tunes will have a few notes at the beginning of a section of tune which don't appear to be part of a whole bar:

These notes, called **pick-up notes** or **lead notes**, aren't extra notes - they usually belong to the bar at the end of the previous section, or to the bar at the end of the following section.

TUNES WITH BARS OF DIFFERENT LENGTHS

Very occasionally tunes will have a bar or two which have a different time signature to the rest of the tune. The new time signature is shown at the start of the relevant bar or bars, and the original time signature is shown when the bars revert back to the first rhythm, for example:

SOME TIME SIGNATURES LOOK THE SAME...

Some time signatures, like 3/4 and 6/8, look as if they are exactly the same and should be interchangeable, but in fact they allow us to write down different kinds of rhythm.

A bar of **3/4** (three crotchets) can be divided into quavers, but the quavers are always grouped within the three crotchet structure, maintaining the three beats in the bar:

In a bar of **6/8** (six quavers), the quavers can be grouped in any way but are most commonly seen in two groups of three, which means that there are two main beats in the bar (impossible to write down in 3/4):

Bars of quavers are counted according to their groupings (rather than trying to count eight quavers in a bar) so the bar above has two main beats.

It is important to understand that **the time signature doesn't show the overall speed of the tune in any way**. A tune written in 6/8 time may be a slow air, a jig or a march. The speed of a tune will be influenced by many factors, such as your own interpretation or the purpose of a tune (e.g. for dancing). Occasionally tunes have what is called a metronome mark which does indicate speed (see page 22) but remember that this is someone else's interpretation and is not compulsory.

Remember that only notes with flags (tails) can be joined together. The way the notes are joined by beams helps you to understand the basic rhythm of the tune. If you find tunes on the Internet, do be careful - sometimes they've been written down by someone who doesn't fully understand this (or with software which might group the notes differently). Always try to find out about the style of the type of tune you are playing.

TRADITIONAL TUNES AND THEIR TIME SIGNATURES

The following is a selection of some of the western European traditional dance tunes and their time signatures:

2/4: Polka, March, Scottish (mainland Europe), Bourrée, An Dro

3/4: Waltz, Mazurka, Polska, Retreat March, Hanter Dro

4/4: Reel, Hornpipe, Strathspey, Scots Measure, March, Gavotte

3/2: Hornpipe

3/8: Bourrée

6/8: Jig, Muiñeira, March, Dérobée, Tarantella

9/8: Slip Jig

12/8: Slide, Gavotte, Fandango

Each kind of tune has its own style (and dance speed), and some tunes of the same type are played differently in different places (e.g. reels from the Scottish West Highlands and reels from County Clare, Ireland). Some types of tune have different varieties in different time signatures (e.g. hornpipes). Sometimes the same tune can be written in two different time signatures depending on one's interpretation of the rhythm of the tune (e.g. gavotte in 4/4 and 12/8 - both have 4 main beats in the bar but the rhythm is slightly different).

What all this essentially means is that the heart of traditional music can't be fully captured on the page. Part Eight has some suggestions for bringing the tune alive once you have deciphered the written music.

Part Five: Reading Rhythms

Written music contains a lot of information which is difficult to digest all at once. This section offers some suggestions to help the beginner get to grips with the different lengths of notes in a tune.

Listen! Within each different style of traditional music there are rhythmic patterns which will occur again and again. Listen to the good musicians do it and get a feel for the rhythms, both in an overall sense and for specific tunes.

Tap your feet! Get your feet to tap the main beats of the music. This will help to keep you in time. It is easy to get caught up in reading the notes on a page and forget about the beat. Playing or singing is a physical activity and the tune will come out in a more rhythmical way if you can get your body to feel the rhythm in a relaxed manner.

Practice the rhythm on its own. Try just playing or tapping out the rhythm rather than trying to read the different notes at the same time. It is easy to slow down or speed up without realising; having a metronome is a very useful way of keeping in time. You can either buy one or use one online (try the one at www.metronomeonline.com). You will need to choose your speed - try slowly at first and choose a faster speed when you feel more confident. Metronomes use beats per minute, so the lower the number, the slower the pulse. Working with a metronome can be frustrating to start with but it is essential that you learn to keep time.

Think about the beat or pulse of a tune. Practice the rhythm of tunes in 2/4, 3/4 and 4/4 by counting the main beats while tapping out the rhythm. If you're using a metronome, these are the beats it will play to you.

Count: 1   2   1   2   3   1   2   3   4

Practice tunes in 6/8, 9/8 and 12/8 by counting the main beats according to how the notes are grouped: usually in two groups of three in 6/8, three groups of three in 9/8 and four groups of three in 12/8.

1   2   1   2   3   1   2   3   4

Uneven or composite time signatures: these are time signatures that can't be divided up in to equal groups of notes, such as 7/8 or 5/4. Rather than trying to count all the beats, break it down into parts. A tune in 7/8 will either be divided into 3 + 4 or 4 + 3:

Count: 1 2 3   1 2 3 4   1 2 3 4   1 2 3   or
        1 2 3   1 2 1 2   1 2 1 2   1 2 3

Set your metronome to beat time in single quaver beats. Look at how the notes are grouped - this shows you how to count.

Dotted notes and rhythms: count these slowly to start with until they become familiar. It may be helpful to break them down, counting the note lengths using the shortest note as the basic unit.

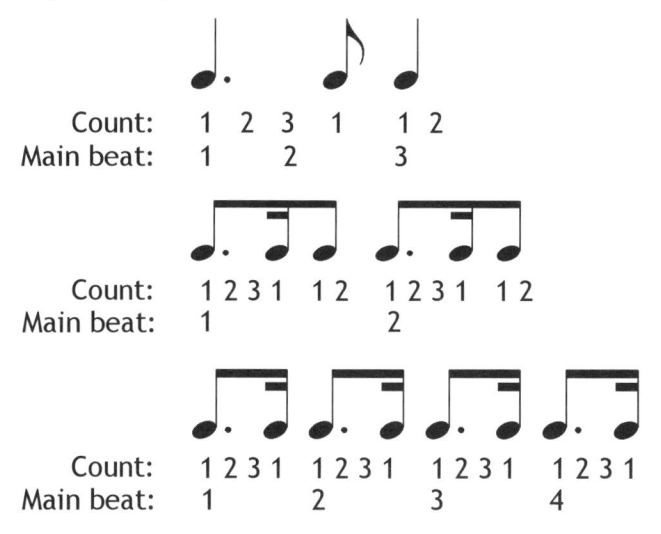

Count: 1 2 3   1   1 2
Main beat: 1   2   3

Count: 1 2 3 1   1 2   1 2 3 1   1 2
Main beat: 1   2

Count: 1 2 3 1   1 2 3 1   1 2 3 1   1 2 3 1
Main beat: 1   2   3   4

Emphasise some notes more that others. It is important to give some rhythmic shape to the notes of a tune. If every note is given the same emphasis, the resulting tune has the potential to sound more like machine gun fire! Different traditions have different rhythmic styles which means that they will emphasise different beats in the bar, but a good starting point is to strongly emphasise the first note in each bar and lightly emphasise the remaining main beats.

part six: which notes to play

KEYS AND SCALES

Not all the notes from the Keyboard 3 diagram on page 3 are used in every piece of music; each tune uses a selection of specific notes which follows a pattern. This pattern of notes is the **key** of a tune. It is helpful to know which notes are used in the common keys in traditional music (see page 18). If you are learning a tune by ear, this gives you a basic structure for the tune. This basic structure is also very useful if you are accompanying tunes as it will help you to decide on appropriate chords.

The notes in a particular key are found using a selection of notes called a **scale**. A scale is a series of notes which are like the rungs on a ladder.

There are two main types of key, **major** and **minor**, and for each of these two types of key there is a specific scale of notes, moving upwards in specific patterns of tones and semitones.

THE MAJOR SCALE

Each rung on the diagram opposite represents a note in the scale. Remember that a tone equals two semitones.

A scale can start on any note and it moves upwards in the pattern shown until it reaches the note of the same name which is an octave above.

The starting note (known as the root note or tonic) gives the scale its name, e.g. C major or D major, and scales have the same notes in every octave.

The examples on the next page are only written in one octave, but the pattern applies in any octave using the same notes.

When musicians refer to major scales and keys, they often miss out the word "major". So if someone tells you that the tune is in D, they are likely to mean D major (i.e. the tune uses the notes of the scale of D major).

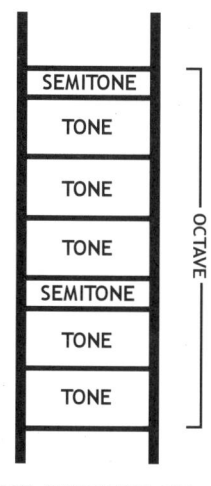

**THE PATTERN OF
THE MAJOR SCALE**

The scale of C major uses all the white notes on the piano keyboard (i.e. it uses no sharps or flats to raise or lower the basic notes) and is written like this in the treble clef:

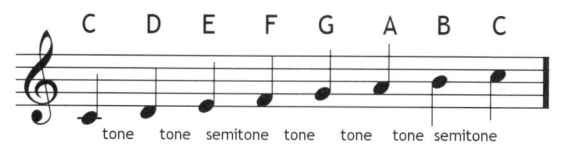

C D E F G A B C
tone tone semitone tone tone tone semitone

The scale of G major has one note sharpened (F#) and is written like this in the treble clef:

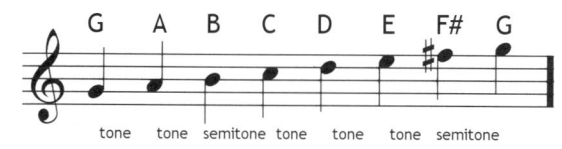

G A B C D E F# G
tone tone semitone tone tone tone semitone

There are also scales which use flats - the scale of F major has one flat (B♭):

F G A B♭ C D E F
tone tone semitone tone tone tone semitone

THE NATURAL MINOR SCALE

There are several different minor scales; the natural minor is the scale closest to the notes of the minor keys most often used by traditional musicians in western Europe (see page 20 for some of the common exceptions). As you will see from the diagram below, the natural minor follows a different pattern to that of the major scale.

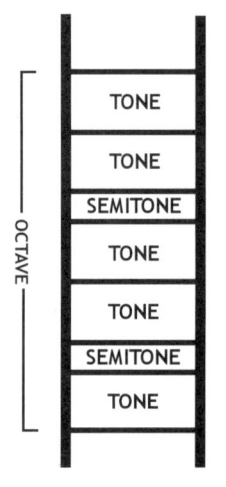

The ladder pattern (top to bottom): TONE, TONE, SEMITONE, TONE, TONE, SEMITONE, TONE — spanning one OCTAVE.

THE PATTERN OF THE NATURAL MINOR SCALE

When talking about the key of a tune, most people won't mention "natural" minor. They will say that a tune is in A minor or E minor. Check which notes are used in the tune.

The scale of A natural minor has no sharps or flats:

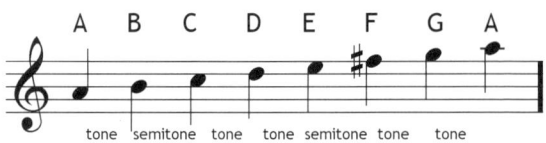

A B C D E F G A
tone semitone tone tone semitone tone tone

The scale of E natural minor has one sharp (F#):

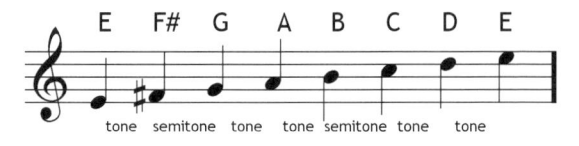

E F# G A B C D E
tone semitone tone tone semitone tone tone

The scale of D natural minor has one flat (B♭):

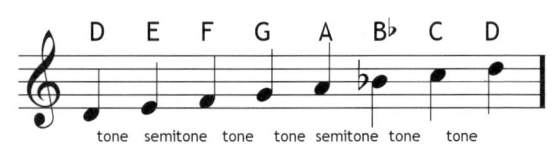

D E F G A B♭ C D
tone semitone tone tone semitone tone tone

KEY SIGNATURES

To make music less cluttered, the sharps or flats which show the key of a tune are written at the beginning of each stave, and they apply to all the notes in the tune. They also apply to all the notes of the same name - in the example below the F# in the key signature is written on the top line of the stave, but all F notes are sharpened, not just the F written on the top line. This shorthand way of writing these sharps or flats is called the **key signature**.

As long as you follow the instructions given by the key signature, you will use the correct notes, but it can be helpful to know the key of a tune, especially so that you can give instructions about the tune to other musicians.

As you can work out from the scales shown on the previous pages, each major scale has an equivalent minor scale which uses the same notes (see the C major and A natural minor scales). The equivalent minor scale is called the **relative minor**. This means that from the key signature alone you can't tell whether the key is major or minor. You can guess from the sound of the tune, and often (but not always) tunes end on the root or first note of the scale.

COMMON KEY SIGNATURES IN TRADITIONAL MUSIC

MAJOR KEY	RELATIVE MINOR	SHARPS/FLATS	KEY SIGNATURE
C major	A minor	None	
G major	E minor	F#	
D major	B minor	F#, C#	
A major	F# minor	F#, C#, G#	
E major	C# minor	F#, C#, G#, D#	
F major	D minor	B♭	
B♭ major	G minor	B♭, E♭	

ACCIDENTALS

Sometimes notes which don't belong to the key of a tune will appear, and these will have a sharp, flat or natural sign next to them. A note occuring in the music which has one of these symbols beside it is called an **accidental**. This instruction **applies to all the notes of that pitch in the whole bar** (but not notes of the same name which are an octave higher or lower) unless it is cancelled out by another symbol. In the example below, the key signature is 2 sharps, F# and C# (the key of D major). The C in the second bar is turned into a C natural, and this applies to the next C in that bar as well, but reverts to C# in the next bar.

C#   C♮   C♮   C#

SOME EXCEPTIONS

The scales used in traditional music don't always match those of classical music, and the differences aren't always written in the same way. An example of this in a major scale is the highland bagpipe scale. This has all the notes of the scale of A major except that the G is natural and not sharp. (To dig deeper into this complex issue, see suggestions for further investigation on page 20.) The key signature of a tune which has come from the bagpipe repertoire might be written in 3 different ways:

With the standard A major key signature and all Gs in the tune marked with a natural

With the G natural shown in the key signature, implying that the G sharp has been changed to a G natural but the key is still A major

With any reference to the G left out - be careful, this looks like D major!

This information doesn't necessarily affect your reading of the tune (the notes will be right) but will be critical to your accompanist - they may start playing D major chords which don't fit!

A common exception in the natural minor scale is that the sixth note of the scale is often a semitone higher, which means that:
- a tune in A minor (which normally has no sharps or flats) may have an F# instead of an F;
- a tune in E minor may have a C# instead of a C;
- a tune in B minor may have a G# instead of a G.

You may find these extra sharps added to the notes in the tune, or you may find them in the key signature.

Key signatures in classical music are made up of either sharps or flats and not a mixture of the two. You may find some traditional tunes which do have both sharps and flats in the key signature - just follow the instructions!

for further investigation...

KEY SIGNATURES

There are more key signatures than are shown on page 18. Look up the **Circle of Fifths** to see all the keys and their relationship to each other.

SCALES AND MODES

As well as the fixed pattern of scales, there are patterns of notes called **modes** which are different ways of organising the basic scale. Often traditional tunes can be explained more successfully using modes when they don't fit the standard classical major or minor scale patterns.

Classical music also uses two further minor scales, the **harmonic minor** and the **melodic minor**.

Some traditional tunes actually use scales which leave out some of the notes in the scale. This won't be immediately obvious when reading the tune on the page, but you may discover a note or notes which are never used. This will be important if you start trying out your own variations in a tune. One of the most common is the **pentatonic scale** which only uses five notes per octave. There are several versions which use different groups of five notes.

Part Seven: Other Symbols

Here is a selection of the other symbols you will find in written music.

REPEAT MARKS: many traditional tunes are written in several parts, each part being repeated once before moving on to the next section. The repeat symbols ||: and :|| surround the part to be repeated:

Often in written traditional music the "start repeat" mark is left out. If you can't find it, repeat the section of the tune which comes before the "end repeat" mark.

Other similar symbols are ‖ which shows the end of a section of music, and ‖ which shows the end of the whole tune.

FIRST AND SECOND ENDINGS: many tunes have a slight change in the ending when a section is repeated. To avoid writing the whole part again, written music uses first and second endings to show which bars to change.

In this example you should play the first four bars, go back to the beginning and play the first three bars and the fifth bar (the alternative ending). First and second endings can contain more than one bar.

TIES AND SLURS: these symbols look the same but are different!

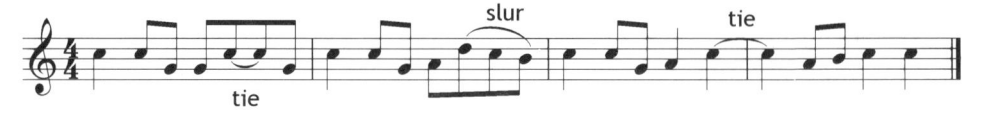

A **tie** joins two notes of the same pitch together, and these notes should be played as one long note. A **slur** joins different notes together, and is normally an indication of a style of playing. It often means that the notes should be played smoothly together with an emphasis on the first note, and can be used as an instruction to players of specific instruments. For example, fiddle players would play the three notes joined by the slur using only one bow stroke.

OTHER SYMBOLS

Several have the Italian names which are used in classical music. Remember that they may be from someone else's style of playing. Some of these symbols are ornaments or grace notes, and the exact playing of these will depend on the which tradition they're from and the instrument on which they're played.

> \>   *accent* - emphasise this note (written above or below the note)
>
> •   *staccato* - a short, detatched note (written above or below the note)
>
> ⟨   *crescendo* - get louder
>
> ⟩   *decrescendo* - get quieter
>
> ⊓ V   *down bow* and *up bow* - instructions to fiddlers
>
> ⌒   *pause* - hold this note for longer than usual
>
> ♪   *grace notes* - the grace note with a line through the stem is technically shorter than the note without the line through it in classical music, but this will depend on the style of the tune
>
> ∽   *roll* or *turn* - ornament
>
> *tr*   *trill* - ornament
>
> ♩ = 120   *metronome mark* - the suggested speed for the tune, in this case 120 crotchet beats per minute
>
> **A, Em, D7** etc.   *chord names* - written above or below the tune, suggested chords for accompanists
>
> *pp, p, mp, mf, f, ff*   *volume instructions* - these stand for: very soft (*pianissimo*); soft (*piano*); moderately soft (*mezzo piano*); moderately loud (*mezzo forte*); loud (*forte*); and very loud (*fortissimo*)
>
> '   *take a breath here* - often found in music for whistle and flute, written above the music
>
> 𝄋 *Dal Segno, D.S.*   Dal Segno means "from the sign" and is an instruction to repeat the music from the 𝄋 sign
>
> *Da Capo, D.C.*   Da Capo means "from the beginning", so go back to the start of the music
>
> *Fine*   Fine means "end" and is written where the whole piece should finish if it doesn't finish at the end of the written music. *Dal Segno al Fine* means "play from the sign to where *fine* is written" and *Da Capo al Fine* means "play from the beginning to *fine*"

part 8: what next?

Reading the right notes in the right rhythms from the page is only the first stage of interpreting the tune. This section looks at some of the limits of written music and suggests ways of moving beyond the manuscript. If you have just started learning how to play or sing, keep working on the basics but bear these ideas in mind for the future.

DOES IT SOUND RIGHT?

Don't always trust the written music, especially if you've found it on the Internet. That odd note in the second part may not come from the composer's jazz influence or the way they played the tune in the eighteenth century - it may be a typing error! Find another version or ask someone if you're not sure.

DOES IT FEEL RIGHT?

It can be difficult to decide on the right time signature when writing out a tune. In the list of tunes and time signatures on page 12, the Gavotte (a Breton dance) is found in both 4/4 and 12/8 time, not necessarily because there are two distinct versions of the tune but because different people have written it down in different ways. The time signature (for some tunes) and the lengths of the notes themselves are only approximations of what has been heard.

LISTEN TO THE STYLE!

These little differences in note lengths are part of the bigger picture of a tune. As I mentioned in the introduction, the tune on paper is just the skeleton of something more complex. Listen to the style of good players and singers - this will give you a sense of the timing of the tune and the kind of extras which bring it to life. Find out about the ornamentation (the twiddly bits!) of the style or styles you want to play. Think about the phrasing of the tune - how it may rise and fall in volume, emphasis and (sometimes) speed. Remember that styles can vary not only from one region to another but even from one village to another. This may seem a daunting task, but don't let this put you off. It's a gradual process which lasts a lifetime for everyone! There are more and more workshops on offer now, and plenty of CDs available.

THROW AWAY THE MUSIC!

Try to memorise the tune. It may help to try breaking it down into sections. This process may be hard to begin with but you will get better at learning tunes as you learn more of them because familiar patterns will start to emerge. If you are able to do this, you will find it easier to do a number of things...

BRING IN THE STYLE: you can experiment with all the aspects of style and the technical skills they require. In particular, it is much easier to play around with the the overall phrasing and rhythm of a tune if your brain isn't trying to read individual notes.

VERSIONS AND VARIATIONS: the tune on paper is only one version of the tune. Just as witnesses to a crime all have a slighly different version of events, the transcriber of a tune will have written down their own interpretation. You can find several different versions, or you can try out your own variations - this is positively encouraged in traditional music and is part of its continuing evolution. Again, your brain will struggle to be creative with the tune if it is reading the notes on the page.

PLAYING WITH OTHERS: playing from memory allows you to engage fully with the other musicians around you. This is important in many subtle ways, but it is also critical in a number of basic areas. You should all be playing or singing the same tune (or harmonies) at the same speed. This sounds obvious but doesn't always happen! If you are playing a set of tunes, it is helpful for everyone to nod, wink or smile at each other when the next tune is coming up. Someone may want to give an instruction or a signal meaning "sing the chorus again" which you will miss if your eyes are glued to the paper.

It is worth experimenting with the tactics which work for you. For instance, there are several people I know who have written down the first couple of bars of lots of tunes, and this helps to jog their memory.

ENJOY YOURSELF!

The music will sound so much better.

Index

Accent.....................................22	Minor scale....................15, 17-18, 20
Accidentals............................19	Modes.....................................20
Bars..9	Natural....................................3
Bass clef.................................5	Natural minor scale........15, 17-18, 20
Beams...............................7, 11	Note names..........................1-4, 6
C clef......................................5	Octave.....................................1
Clefs..5	Ornamentation....................22, 23
Common time.........................9	
Crotchet..................................7	Pause.....................................22
Crescendo.............................22	Pianissimo.............................22
Cut time..................................9	Piano.....................................22
	Pick-up notes.........................10
Da Capo................................22	
Dal Segno.............................22	Quarter note...........................7
Decrescendo.........................22	Quaver....................................7
Dotted notes...........................8	
	Relative minor.......................18
Eighth note.............................7	Repeats..................................21
Endings.................................21	Rests..8
	Rhythms............................13-14
Fine.......................................22	Roll..22
Flat..3	
Forte.....................................22	Scale.................................15-20
Fortissimo.............................22	Semibreve...............................7
	Semiquaver............................7
Grace notes..........................22	Semitone.................................2
	Sharp......................................3
Half note.................................7	Sixteenth note.........................7
	Slur..21
Key..................................15-20	Staccato.................................22
Key signature...................18-20	Staff, stave..............................5
Lead notes............................10	Tie...21
Leger lines..............................6	Time signature..............9-12, 13-14
	Tone..2
Major scale......................15-16	Treble clef...............................5
Metronome mark............11, 22	Trill.......................................22
Mezzo forte..........................22	Triplet.....................................8
Mezzo piano.........................22	Turn.......................................22
Middle C.................................6	
Minim......................................7	Whole note..............................7